Dear Parent:

Buckle up! You are about to join your child on a very exciting journey. The destination? Independent reading!

Road to Reading will help you and your child get there. The program offers books at five levels, or Miles, that accompany children from their first attempts at reading to successfully reading on their own. Each Mile is paved with engaging stories and delightful artwork.

Getting Started
For children who know the alphabet and are eager to begin reading
• easy words • fun rhythms • big type • picture clues

Reading With Help
For children who recognize some words and sound out others with help
• short sentences • pattern stories • simple plotlines

Reading On Your Own
For children who are ready to read easy stories by themselves
• longer sentences • more complex plotlines • easy dialogue

First Chapter Books
For children who want to take the plunge into chapter books
• bite-size chapters • short paragraphs • full-color art

Chapter Books
For children who are comfortable reading independently
• longer chapters • occasional black-and-white illustrations

There's no need to hurry through the Miles. Road to Reading is designed without age or grade levels. Children can progress at their own speed, developing confidence and pride in their reading ability no matter what their age or grade.

So sit back and enjoy the ride—

D1057777

For Barbara, Cheryl, and Terry
M.M.

For Anita
A.W.

Library of Congress Cataloging-in-Publication Data
McDonald, Megan.
Lucky star / by Megan McDonald ; illustrated by Andréa Wallace.
 p.   cm. — (Road to reading. Mile 3)
Summary: Star cannot wait to share her library book with her best friend
Blister, but when the book gets ruined, they get into a fight over it.
ISBN 0-307-46329-X (hardbound). — ISBN 0-307-26329-0 (pbk.)
[1. Friendship Fiction.   2. Books and reading Fiction.]   I. Wallace, Andréa,
ill. II. Title. III. Series.
PZ7.M478419Lu 2000
[E]—dc21   99-24652
                                                            CIP

A GOLDEN BOOK • New York
Golden Books Publishing Company, Inc. New York, New York 10106

Lucky Star

by Megan McDonald
illustrated by Andréa Wallace

THE SMUDGE

Star liked to find rocks.

Star liked to paint.

Star liked to read, read, read.

Star's baby-sitter, Jill,

took her to the library.

Just Star.

Not her big sister, Ivy.

Star got a brand-new
library card like Ivy's.
Star got a sticker that said,
"I got carded at the library."
She put the sticker on her hand.
She put the sticker on her shoe.
She put the sticker on her forehead.

"Pick out a book," said Jill.

Star picked out a brand-new book

about a cat who ate pizza.

Pepperoni pizza.

Star read the book
all the way
down the sidewalk.
She forgot to look for rocks.

Star read the book
right past Quick Pix.
She forgot to ask Jill
for glitter paints.

Star read the book to Jill
all the way home.

Star read the book

through the fence

to Mrs. Ling's corn.

She read to Mrs. Ling's beans.

She read to Mrs. Ling's cat.

"Meow," said Jasper.

"Jasper likes this book!" said Jill.

"Blister will like this book, too!"

said Star.

Star found her friend Blister

eating pizza.

Pepperoni pizza.

So Star and Blister

ate pizza like cats

and read the new book together.

"Turn the page," said Blister,
with two hands full of pizza.
"You turn the page," said Star,
with two hands full of pizza.
Blister turned the page.

"Oh no!" cried Star.

"Oh no!" cried Blister.

The brand-new clean white page

had a big orange pizza thumbprint!

14

Star wiped the thumbprint
with a napkin.
Now the thumbprint
was a big orange smudge.

Blister wiped the big orange smudge with a wet sponge.

Now the book was all wet.

Blister dried the book with a towel.

Now the page was wrinkled.

"Let's erase it!" said Blister.

Star and Blister erased

the big orange wet wrinkled smudge.

The smudge got even more smudgey.

Star and Blister erased some more.

Star and Blister ripped the page!

"You broke it!" said Star.

"You broke it!" said Blister.

"It's your thumbprint!" said Star.

"You made me turn the page!"
said Blister.

Star went home mad.

Blister went to his room mad.

Star showed Jill the page that ripped.

"I'm telling," said Ivy.

Poison Ivy, thought Star.

Jill said Star would have to pay
for the book.

"How much will it cost?" asked Star.

"Ten dollars," said Jill.

"Ten dollars!" yelled Ivy.

"Star doesn't even have ten cents!"

Star did have ten cents.

But she did not have ten dollars.

So Star went looking for ten dollars.

TEN DOLLARS

Star looked on the porch.

Star looked under the steps.

Star looked in sidewalk cracks.

Star found a button,

a cat's-eye marble,

a hair clip, and a rusty nail.

But she did not find ten dollars.

Star looked through the fence
at Mrs. Ling's garden.
WEEDS!
Weeds gave Star an idea.

She asked Mrs. Ling
if she could weed her garden
to earn some money.
"A dollar a pile!" said Mrs. Ling.

Star pulled at a weed.

Weeds! Weeds! Weeds!

She dug up a root.

She tore out a blade of grass.

Ten cents' worth of weeds.

"Ten dollars takes forever!" said Star.

"Watch out for poison ivy!"

yelled Ivy through the fence.

"You mean YOU," said Star.

Blister looked through the fence.

"I'm still mad," he called.

"I'm still mad, too," called Star.

Blister came over.

Star and Blister madly pulled up weeds.

They pulled one two three weeds.

Four five six.

Seven eight nine ten.

Blister pulled weeds

until he had a blister on his thumb.

He threw the weeds in small piles.

Star never knew

Blister was so good at weeds.

"Are you still mad?" asked Star.

"I'm still mad," said Blister.

"Me, too," said Star.

Star tugged on stems.

She yanked out vines.

Star pulled weeds

until she had two blisters.

"Are you still mad?" asked Blister.

"Yes," said Star.

They pulled weeds faster and faster,

madder and madder.

Small weeds, tall weeds.

Jaggy weeds, shaggy weeds.

Now Blister had one two three blisters.

"Three is a lot of blisters," said Blister.

"And I already had one.

Four is even more."

"Let's count weed piles," said Star.

"Let's count blisters!" said Blister.

Star and Blister counted.

Star and Blister forgot

about being mad.

They piled their weeds together.

"That's what I call
a six-blister hill of weeds!"
said Blister.
"A ten-dollar mountain of weeds!"
said Star.

SIDEWALK SALE

Star and Blister went to the library
to pay back the ten dollars.
On the way they stopped at Quick Pix.
Star wished she could
buy a butterfly yo-yo.
Blister wished he could
buy a Wiz Bang top.
"Let's get out of here," said Star.
"Before we spend the ten dollars!"
said Blister.

Star and Blister ran
all the way to the library
and paid the ten dollars.
The library was selling old books
on the sidewalk.
"We could have a sale, too," said Star.
"Then I could buy a butterfly yo-yo."

"I could buy a Wiz Bang top!"
said Blister.

"No more blisters!"
said Star and Blister.

So Star and Blister
held a sidewalk sale.
Blister had a penny,
a deck of old cards,
ugly bug stickers,
and a snow globe with no snow.

Star had a rock,
a trouble doll,
and a picture she painted
of a chocolate chip cookie.
She had a button,
a cat's-eye marble, a hair clip,
and a rusty nail.

Star and Blister made signs.

Star and Blister made price tags.

Ivy came to the sidewalk sale.

"How much for the penny?"

Ivy asked Blister.

"Two cents," said Blister.

"Ha, ha," said Ivy.

She bought three ugly bug stickers.

"Hey!" said Ivy. "That's my hair clip!

And my button and my cat's-eye!"

"Is this your rusty nail, too?" asked Star.

"Ha, ha," said Ivy.

"Look! A trouble doll!" Ivy said.

"They keep away trouble."

Star wanted to keep away trouble.

Like sisters.

And broken library books.

"It's not for sale," she said.

Up came Jill with little Luke.

"I baby-sit Luke every Saturday," said Jill.

"I brought him to your sidewalk sale."

Jill bought Blister's deck of cards

and the snow globe with no snow.

Luke bought Blister's penny

for two cents.

Jill picked up Star's cookie painting.

"This is art," said Jill.

"I've been looking for some art
to hang on my fridge."

Star wanted to hang art
on her fridge, too.

"It's not for sale," said Star.

Jill picked up the rock.

"A lucky stone," said Jill.

"I'll buy it."

Star did not know her rock was lucky.

Star needed good luck.

"It's not for sale," said Star.

Blister went to get more things to sell.

He brought back comic books,

a shell, and two pencils

with teeth marks.

He sold those, too.

"Blister," said Star,

"you could sell the blister

right off your thumb."

Blister counted his money.

"Wow!" said Blister.

"Now I can buy a Wiz Bang top!"

He looked at Star's table.

"You did not sell one thing!"

said Blister.

"How will you buy

a butterfly yo-yo?"

"I have something better," said Star.

"Better than a butterfly yo-yo?"

asked Blister.

"I have art!" said Star.

"I have good luck.

And I will never have trouble again."